A **TRUE** BOOK

W9-BBC-571

The Pueblo

DISCARD

**KEVIN CUNNINGHAM
AND PETER BENOIT**

Children's Press®
An Imprint of Scholastic Inc.
New York Toronto London Auckland Sydney
Mexico City New Delhi Hong Kong
Danbury, Connecticut

Content Consultant

Scott Manning Stevens, PhD

Director, McNickle Center

Newberry Library

Chicago, Illinois

Library of Congress Cataloging-in-Publication Data

Cunningham, Kevin, 1966–
    The Pueblo/Kevin Cunningham and Peter Benoit.
        p. cm. — (A true book)
    Includes bibliographical references and index.
    ISBN-13: 978-0-531-20763-5 (lib. bdg.)   978-0-531-29305-8 (pbk.)
    ISBN-10: 0-531-20763-3 (lib. bdg.)   0-531-29305-X (pbk.)
1. Pueblo Indians—Juvenile literature. 2. Indians of North America—Southwest, New—Juvenile
literature. I. Benoit, Peter, 1955– II. Title.
    E99.P9C849 2011
    978.9004'974—dc22   2010050838

All rights reserved. Published in 2011 by Children's Press, an imprint of Scholastic Inc.
Printed in China 62
SCHOLASTIC, CHILDREN'S PRESS, A TRUE BOOK and associated logos are trademarks and/or registered trademarks of Scholastic Inc.

1 2 3 4 5 6 7 8 9 10 R 19 18 17 16 15 14 13 12 11

Find the Truth!

Everything you are about to read is true *except* for one of the sentences on this page.

Which one is **TRUE**?

T or F The Pueblo people built a great road that seems to lead to nowhere.

T or F All Pueblos joined together to revolt against the Spanish in 1680.

Find the answers in this book.

Contents

THE **BIG** TRUTH!

**Ancestral Puebloan
cliff dwelling**

4

Popé, organizer of
the Pueblo Revolt

4 Kachinas and Clowns

5 Pueblo History Since the Revolt

Pueblos often used
ponderosa pines to
support kiva roofs.

5

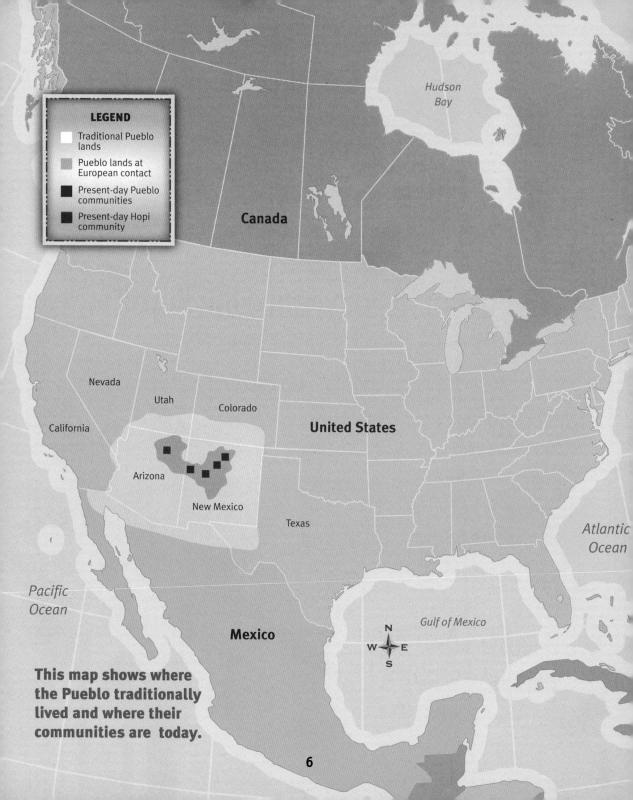

LEGEND

- Traditional Pueblo lands
- Pueblo lands at European contact
- Present-day Pueblo communities
- Present-day Hopi community

Hudson Bay

Canada

Nevada

Utah

Colorado

California

United States

Arizona

New Mexico

Texas

Pacific Ocean

Atlantic Ocean

Mexico

Gulf of Mexico

N
W E
S

This map shows where the Pueblo traditionally lived and where their communities are today.

CHAPTER 1

Both One and Many

Hundreds of years ago, the ancestors of the Hopi, the Zuni, and 19 other Native American groups lived in the southwest United States and Texas. They lived in permanent villages in buildings that they made of clay or dug underground. In the 1500s, Spanish explorers and settlers encountered these well-organized towns. Impressed, the Spanish labeled the people with their word for "village" —*pueblo*. Today, the name *Pueblo* refers to the descendants of these Native American groups.

← *Hopi* means "peaceful person" in the Hopi language.

Masters of Trade

Pueblos developed a system for trading goods with one another. In time, they opened trade with non-Pueblo tribes such as the nearby Navajo, a farming people, and the Comanche, the fierce horseback **raiders** of the Great Plains. Food was one of the Pueblo's most important products. For centuries, they had been raising maize (corn), beans, and squash. They had also acquired turkeys from peoples living in what is now Mexico.

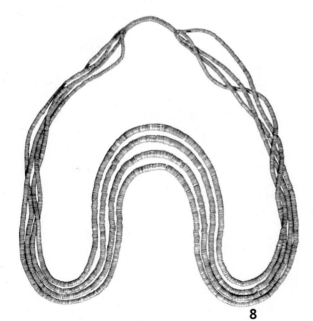

Turquoise, often used for jewelry, was a common trade item with people as far south as Central America.

The Pueblo used farming tools of bone, wood, or stone.

Maize, beans, and squash were important parts of the Pueblo diet.

Desert Farmers

Early in their history, Pueblo peoples hunted deer, rabbit, bear, and other animals for meat and skins. They also fished and gathered wild nuts and fruits. As farming became more important, however, gathering food became less necessary. Meat, too, could be acquired through trade. The Comanche, for instance, offered bison (buffalo) meat and skins in exchange for maize. Needing to stay near their farms, Pueblos began settling down into permanent villages.

Communities grew in size as the Pueblo became more settled.

The southwestern climate is very dry. But in the spring, melting mountain snows flow into the lowlands. The Pueblo borrowed their ancestors' ways by using an **irrigation** system built around a series of dams. The dams trapped the water in man-made lakes so that it could be used later for crops. The Pueblo also planted in places where water ran off after storms. These methods worked so well that some Pueblos farmed cotton, a plant that needs a great deal of water.

In Case of Emergency

The weather turned even drier at times, however. When Pueblo farmers faced **drought**, their inability to grow enough food forced them to look for new farmland. Because the Pueblo also fought other peoples, violence sometimes drove them to move. The Apache and Navajo, for instance, raided Pueblo villages. Later, the Pueblo clashed with the Spanish. In times of trouble, Pueblos might move to the top of a flat-topped hill called a **mesa**.

People have lived in Acoma Pueblo since at least 1200 C.E.

Acoma Pueblo in New Mexico is also called Sky City.

Differences

Though the Pueblo groups share many traits, each one is different. The various Pueblo languages, for example, come from four language families. The various Pueblo groups have their own religious beliefs. Some believe their people rose from the water. Others say their ancestors climbed up from deep inside the earth into the present world. These kinds of differences lead **archaeologists** to think that many peoples blended into the one we call the Pueblo. They were grouped together not because they had the same ancestors, but because they all lived in similar types of homes.

Archaeologists date the Tyuonyi Pueblo ruins in New Mexico to before the 14th century.

Archaeologists use pottery pieces, wood, and building ruins as clues to help them reconstruct a culture.

What's in a Name?

Archaeologists take care not to repeat old and insulting terms. For example, experts believe that two ancient peoples eventually became part of the Pueblo. For a long time, archaeologists called these peoples the Anasazi and the Mogollon. But in recent years, some have begun to use the terms *Ancient Puebloans* or *Ancient Pueblo peoples* instead. Why? Modern Pueblos dislike the term *Anasazi.* It's a Navajo word that can mean "ancient enemies."

Ancient Puebloans are also sometimes called Cliff Dwellers. Towns were often built into the side of a cliff.

The Spanish conquered
Hawikuh in 1540.

14

CHAPTER 2

Religion, Raids, and Revolt

Pueblo peoples first met Europeans when a scouting party led by Estevanico, an African working as a scout for the Spanish, visited the Zuni in 1539. Spanish soldiers arrived the next year. Spanish officials tried to force Pueblos to give up their **traditional** beliefs and become Catholic. Often, Pueblos killed the men sent to make them take up the new faith. The Spanish tortured Pueblos for resisting change.

Hawikuh was the first pueblo that Spanish explorers found.

Pueblo people farmed land for the Spanish in return for the protection of the Spanish soldiers.

The Work System

The king of Spain gave Indian land to explorers and soldiers. As part of a work system called the **encomienda**, Spanish landowners took charge of the Pueblo people and promised protection. In return, Pueblos agreed to work and grow food for the Spaniards. At first, many Pueblos went along. Their Apache and Navajo enemies had become deadlier than ever since they had gotten horses. The Spanish, however, could fight them off.

Hard Times

Spaniards forced the Pueblo into slavery. The combination of the harsh encomienda and the attacks against their religion made Pueblos feel that their **independence** and way of life were slipping away. Then drought gripped the Southwest in the 1670s. The lack of food soon made the problem of raids worse than ever. When the Spanish failed to stop the raids, many Pueblos felt they had broken their promises.

Europeans brought the first horses to the Americas in 1493.

Native Americans sometimes raided villages to take livestock or stored grains.

Arrest of the Medicine Men

European diseases also struck the Pueblo people. Needing comfort in hard times, Pueblos turned back to their religion. Catholic officials, angry at Pueblo stubbornness, decided to get rid of the Pueblo religion for good. Spaniards burned the ceremonial dolls, prayer sticks, and masks the Pueblo used in their **rituals**. Prayer dances were forbidden. Finally, the Spanish governor arrested 47 Pueblo holy men, or medicine men, for witchcraft. After whipping and jailing all of them, he had four hanged.

The Spanish banned traditional Pueblo ceremonies such as the Dance of the Great Knife.

Popé's Plans

Threats of war from furious Pueblo warriors forced the Spanish to free the rest of the medicine men. One of them was an Ohkay Owingeh (o-WEENG-eh) Pueblo named Popé (po-PAY). He spent the next five years planning a **revolt** against the Spanish. Not all the Pueblo groups joined the revolt, but most did. Popé's rebels overcame huge problems such as language differences among the native groups and the long distances between their villages. They also kept their plans a secret.

Popé hid in a village near modern-day Taos, New Mexico.

A statue of Popé stands in the National Statuary Hall in the U.S. Capitol in Washington, D.C.

Most Spaniards fled to Santa Fe or Isleta one day after the Pueblos' first attack.

The Pueblo Revolt

To prepare for the attack, Pueblo leaders sent, runners carrying knotted cords with coded messages to other leaders. On August 10, 1680, 8,000 Pueblo warriors surprised Spanish forces all across New Mexico. They soon killed more than 400 Spaniards. The Spanish survivors retreated to Santa Fe, the only Spanish city in the region, or to Isleta, a village that had refused to revolt.

The Pueblo warriors followed the Spaniards to Santa Fe and surrounded the city. By late August, the 3,000 or so people trapped inside could no longer get fresh water. Unable to hold out, the Spaniards killed their Pueblo prisoners and broke out of the city. The Pueblos let the Spanish go. It was enough that they had taken back their homeland. The victory, however, did not last long.

Pueblos destroyed many of the churches built by Spanish missionaries.

The church at San Geronimo Mission in Taos was one of many churches destroyed in the Pueblo Revolt.

Europeans first settled in Santa Fe in 1598, nine years before the English settled Jamestown, Virginia.

The peaceful agreement between Diego de Vargas and the Pueblos is celebrated with a festival each year in Santa Fe.

The Spanish Return

Popé angered many of his people by demanding they reject Spanish ways. Pueblo leaders also disagreed about who would rule. At the same time, the drought continued. Apache and Navajo raiders rode in again and again. In 1692, the Spanish official Diego de Vargas asked to meet with Pueblo leaders. He promised protection and agreed to not punish Pueblo rebels if the Spanish could return. In September of that year, the Pueblo gave Santa Fe back to the Spanish.

The Pueblo revolted again in 1693 and 1696. The Spanish answered by burning villages and killing and enslaving Pueblos. But the Spaniards eventually eased the violence. Officials eager for peace backed off attacking the Pueblo religion and traditions. Instead, they got rid of encomienda, gave land to Pueblos, and learned to ignore the Pueblo faith. The revolts, though unsuccessful in the end, had given the Pueblo a chance to keep their way of life.

The revolts eventually allowed the Pueblo people to live more freely.

Many of the structures at Mesa Verde still stand, even though they were built several hundred years ago.

CHAPTER 3

The Pueblo Way of Building

Pueblo **architecture** is famous around the world. Architecture is a style and method of building structures. Travelers today visit the Southwest to see structures hundreds of years old at Mesa Verde and the Gila Cliff Dwellings. Many sites date back more than 700 years to the time of the Pueblos' ancestors. Thanks to the dry desert air, the ruins have held up well.

Mesa Verde in Colorado became a national park in 1906.

The Building Material

The ancient Pueblo peoples built dwellings on cliffs. Their main building materials were stone and **adobe**. To make adobe, the builders mixed sand, clay, and water with straw. For centuries, they packed the adobe mixture by hand to make walls. Later, the Spanish passed on the idea of bricks. After that, Pueblos poured the adobe mixture into a brick-shaped frame, removed the frame, and let the adobe brick dry before using it.

Pueblos add straw to an adobe mixture.

The ancient Pueblo Bonito complex had 800 rooms.

The New Architecture

As time passed, the ancient Pueblos' simpler architecture gave way to large buildings. The largest had four or five stories and hundreds of rooms. Structures built on mesas were reached by rope ladders that people lifted up when enemies approached. Complexes in the flatlands usually had several stories and faced south. Those built on cliffs featured steps carved out of rock to allow people to get around.

The Kiva

Structures known as kivas played a major role in Pueblo religious life. Often built underground, a kiva had a fire pit dug into its floor. In a large adobe village, the Pueblos built one small kiva for every 30 (later 60 or 90) rooms. The Hopi and Zuni preferred square kivas. Others were usually round. A large kiva stretched over 60 feet (18 meters) across.

Link to Other Worlds

A kiva had a hole in the floor called the *sipapu*. It reminded the Pueblo people of how their ancestors had entered the world, from beneath the earth. The Hopi believed their forefathers climbed out of a sipapu in the Grand Canyon.

Members Only

Pueblo peoples only allowed men and boys to enter the kiva. Once they had climbed inside from a hole in the roof, they held religious ceremonies or important meetings.

People entered a kiva by ladder through a hole in the roof.

Ancient roads sometimes led to water sources.

Road Systems

Pueblo villagers built roads by making the rock or soil level or by tearing out plants. Some roads led to water sources. Others connected villages. The largest, built by the Pueblos' ancestors before 1125 C.E., is known today as the Great North Road. Thirty feet (9 m) wide, the Great North Road went straight north for close to 31 miles (50 km). Why it was built, however, remains a mystery.

The Great North Road doesn't lead to a town or anything else. It simply reaches a canyon and stops. Archaeologists wonder if the road had a religious meaning. In Pueblo belief, a northward road carries them to the sipapu where their ancestors entered our world. Ancient Pueblo peoples probably shared beliefs similar to those of later times. So it is possible they traveled on the Great North Road as part of a religious ritual.

The remains of the Great North Road run through Chaco Canyon.

Archaeologists use satellites to spot the ancient roads.

CHAPTER 4

Kachinas and Clowns

Not all Pueblo peoples had the same traditional habits. Among the Hopi and Zuni, for example, a mother passed her land to her daughters. When the daughter got married, her new husband lived with her family. Children became a part of the wife's people, too. Yet in other Pueblo groups, property and children stayed with the men.

← Some Hopi villages have been inhabited since before 1100 C.E.

Tied Together by Faith

All Pueblo peoples, however, had religions that involved kachinas. A kachina was the living spirit form of a certain thing in the world. Thunderstorms, for example, had a kachina. So did an important ancestor. So did maize, the most important crop. In the Pueblo religious faith, showing respect to something's kachina could influence that thing. Pueblos might call on a kachina to bring rain or heal the sick.

Timeline of Pueblo History

1125 C.E.
The Ancient Pueblo use the Great North Road.

1539
The Spanish make contact with the Pueblo.

Every Pueblo people had its own beliefs about kachinas. The Hopi believed the kachinas stayed in the mountains half the year. On the first day of winter, the kachinas came down and joined the Hopi for singing and dancing ceremonies. The dancers belonged to a special kachina society. Each dancer wore a mask of a spirit. Hopis believed kachinas lived among them in the villages until the first day of summer.

The Hopi believed in more than 500 different kachinas.

1680
The Pueblo Revolt occurs.

1700s
Smallpox hits the Southwest.

Kachina Dolls

In Pueblo culture, men carved dolls that represented kachinas from cottonwood. Children often received them from their father or grandfather. The dolls were not toys. Instead, adults used kachina dolls to teach children about Pueblo culture and religion and for worship. When a child grew up, he or she might pass on a powerful doll to his or her own children. Today, collectors pay thousands of dollars for well-made or antique dolls.

A lot of care and concentration goes into making a kachina doll.

Sacred Clowns

Sacred clowns also played an important part in religious life. A sacred clown believed that when he put on a kachina mask, a spirit entered his body. The spirit then acted in silly ways using the clown's body. Humor allowed the Pueblos to laugh at themselves and the challenges they faced. Even as the Pueblos laughed, however, they respected a sacred clown's actions as an important part of the ceremony.

Pueblos called the clowns *koshares* (KO-sha-rays).

This kachina doll represents a sacred clown.

The church in Isleta, destroyed in the Pueblo Revolt, was rebuilt after the Spanish returned. It still stands today.

CHAPTER 5

Pueblo History Since the Revolt

After the 1690s, the Pueblo peoples carved out a place for their traditional way of life. But they faced more challenges. The Spanish had brought European diseases in the 1500s. One of those illnesses, **smallpox,** swept through the Pueblo peoples in the 1700s. In some places, more than half the people died. Raiding increased again, too. Their old enemies the Apache kept it up, as did the Ute and the powerful Comanche.

 The Spanish named Isleta Pueblo. *Isleta* means "little island."

Taken Over by the United States

After the Mexican-American War ended in 1848, the United States took over New Mexico. As American settlers moved west, they pushed the Pueblo peoples off their traditional lands. The U.S. government set aside land called **reservations** for the Pueblo to live on. But Pueblos faced a long, painful period. Diseases battered the villages. Whites stole their land and even dragged their children to schools to make them learn American ways.

Life changed for all native groups as more and more non-Indian settlers moved west.

The village of Oraibi is built on a mesa on the Hopi Reservation in Arizona.

The Hopi Reservation is surrounded by the Navajo Reservation.

The Pueblo Peoples in Modern Times

Since the 1940s, the Pueblo have organized. Doing so has helped them protect their land and end the attacks on their religion and traditions. Today's 35,000 Pueblos live in 21 groups in New Mexico, Arizona, and Texas. The biggest one is the 2,410-square-mile (6,242 sq km) Hopi Indian Reservation in northeastern Arizona.

Today's Pueblo, like many Native Americans, often lack work opportunities and health care. Poverty and poor education are also problems. Jobs include farming and making and selling silver jewelry and pottery. A few groups have opened casinos and hotels. Tradition, however, remains a part of everyday life. Adobe is still used for buildings. Many Pueblos practice the old religions. The Pueblo, in fact, have been more successful than most at holding on to their traditions. ★

Many Pueblo villages have existed for hundreds of years.

Reservations have Pueblo-run businesses, police departments, and schools.

Number of Pueblo groups today: 21

Number of medicine men arrested by the Spanish in 1675: 47

Number of Spaniards killed in the Pueblo Revolt: More than 400

Number of rooms in Pueblo Bonito: 800

Distance builders sometimes carried wood for kivas: More than 50 mi. (80 km)

Diameter of a large kiva: More than 60 ft. (18 m)

Width of the Great North Road: 30 ft. (9 m)

Distance the Great North Road runs north: 31 mi. (50 km)

Number of Pueblo people today: 35,000

Did you find the truth?

(T) The Pueblo people built a great road that seems to lead to nowhere.

(F) All Pueblos joined together to revolt against the Spanish in 1680.

Resources

Books

Bishop, Amanda, and Bobbie Kalman. *Life in a Pueblo*. New York: Crabtree, 2003.

Burgan, Michael. New Mexico. Danbury, CT: Children's Press, 2009.

Croy, Anita. *Ancient Pueblo*. Des Moines, IA: National Geographic, 2007.

Englar, Mary. *The Pueblo*. Mankato, MN: Capstone, 2000.

Gray-Kanatiiosh, Barbara A. *Hopi*. Edina, MN: Checkerboard, 2002.

McIntosh, Kenneth. *Pueblo*. Broomall, PA: Mason Crest, 2003.

Press, Petra. *The Zuni*. Minneapolis: Compass Point, 2002.

Ross, Pamela. *The Pueblo Indians*. Mankato, MN: Capstone, 1999.

St. Lawrence, Genevieve. *The Pueblo and Their History*. Minneapolis: Compass Point, 2005.

Organizations and Web Sites

All Indian Pueblo Council
www.20pueblos.org
Learn how the council is aiding Pueblos and helping preserve the Pueblo way of life.

National Museum of the American Indian
www.nmai.si.edu
See exhibits on the lives and cultures of Native Americans.

Pueblo de Cochiti
www.pueblodecochiti.org
Read about life today on the reservation of the Cochiti Pueblo people of New Mexico.

Places to Visit

Haak'u Museum
Sky City Cultural Center
PO Box 310
Pueblo of Acoma, NM 87034
(800) 747-0181
museum.acomaskycity.org
Study exhibits to learn about the art, beliefs, and history of the Acoma Pueblo people.

Taos Pueblo
PO Box 1846
Taos, NM 87571
(575) 758-1028
www.taospueblo.com
Walk the streets and explore the adobe buildings of one of the oldest Pueblo villages in the Southwest.

Important Words

adobe (uh-DOH-bee)—dried bricks made of clay, sand, water, and straw

archaeologists (ar-kee-OL-uh-jistss)—people who study remains of past times and peoples

drought (DROUT)—a long period of unusually low rainfall

encomienda (en-coh-mee-EHN-duh)—system where Pueblo people worked on Spanish farms in exchange for protection

independence (in-di-PEN-duhnss)—a state of not being controlled by others

irrigation (ir-uh-GAY-shun)—a system of watering crops

mesa (MAY-suh)—a broad, flat-topped hill with steep sides

raiders (RAY-durz) people who make sudden, surprise attacks on other people to steal from them

reservations (rez-ur-VAY-shuhnz)—land set aside for use by Native Americans

revolt (ri-VOHLT)—an organized armed uprising

rituals (RICH-oo-ulz)—religious ceremonies with specific rules

sacred (SAY-krud)—related to religion, or holy

smallpox (SMAWL-poks)—a deadly disease that causes a painful rash and can leave survivors terribly scarred

traditional (treh-DISH-uhn-ul)—referring to established patterns of thought or action passed down from generation to generation

Index

Page numbers in **bold** indicate illustrations

About the Authors

Kevin Cunningham has written more than 40 books on disasters, the history of disease, Native Americans, and other topics. Cunningham lives near Chicago with his wife and young daughter.

Peter Benoit is educated as a mathematician but has many other interests. He has taught and tutored high school and college students for many years, mostly in math and science. He also runs summer workshops for writers and students of literature. Benoit has written more than 2,000 poems. His life has been one committed to learning. He lives in Greenwich, New York.